JN175176

Smiljan Radic

House for the Poem of the Right Angle
Red Stone House

Residential Masterpieces 21
Smiljan Radic
House for the Poem of the Right Angle
Red Stone House

Photographs, text and edited by Yoshio Futagawa
Art direction: Gan Hosoya

Copyright © 2016 A.D.A. EDITA Tokyo Co., Ltd.
3-12-14 Sendagaya, Shibuya-ku, Tokyo 151-0051, Japan
All rights reserved. No part of this publication may be reproduced,
stored in a retrieval system, or transmitted,
in any form or by any means, electronic, mechanical,
photocopying, recording, or otherwise,
without permission in writing from the publisher.

Copyright of photographs
©2016 GA photographers

Printed and bound in Japan

ISBN 978-4-87140-646-8 C1352

Smiljan Radic

House for
the Poem of the Right Angle

Vilches, Chile, 2010-12

Red Stone House

Santiago, Chile, 2009-12

Text and Photographed by Yoshio Futagawa

世界現代住宅全集21

スミリャン・ラディッチ
「直角の詩」のための住宅　2010-12
チリ，ビルチェス

レッド・ストーン・ハウス　2009-12
チリ，サンティアゴ

企画：二川幸夫

撮影・文・編集：二川由夫

感性の深みを刺激する豊かで慎ましい家──二川由夫
Rich and Modest Houses that Inspire the Depth of Senses *by Yoshio Futagawa*

ピノチェトが1973年に起こしたクーデターによる軍事政権は，89年にその終焉を迎えるまで，チリに文化的な歪みを生み，建築の分野においても長い停滞状態を引き起こした。80年代後半からその軍事政権が終焉を迎える頃実務を始めた若い世代の建築家の仕事が，次第に世界的な注目を浴びてくる。その先陣を切ったのが若きマティアス・クロッツであり，彼に続くように，首都サンティアゴのカトリック大学の同級生であったスミリャン・ラディッチや後輩のアレハンドロ・アラヴェナといった1965年前後生まれの建築家たちが，今世紀に入り世界的に知られることとなった。その背景には，当時の世界の建築界を席巻していたポストモダニズムを筆頭にしたイズムの嵐からチリが隔離されており，その間に失なわれていたモダニズム理念の本来向かうべき未来が，ゆっくりと熟成されていったためであった。彼らの仕事は，世界が躍起になって新しい方向性を求めて混沌としていたところに，ローカリティから生まれる世界的なトピックとなった。

　スミリャン・ラディッチはキャリアの初期から多くの住宅を手がけてきたが，その存在は，2010年のヴェネチア・ビエンナーレでのインスタレーション，2014年，ロンドン，サーペンタイン・ギャラリーのパヴィリオン，同年のサンティアゴの電波塔コンペ入選などによって国内外に急速に認知される建築家となった。その作品は時に詩的，文

学的であり，哲学的，コンセプチュアルであり，幾何学的であり，彫刻的，絵画的と様々な側面をもつが，それらは彼の引き出しの多いデザインの「上手さ」に常に裏付けられて，手がかりとなる建築の周辺に漂う現象と巧みに付き合うことで豊かな空間が創出されている。この豊かさとは，新しく特殊な体験によって獲得される類のものではなく，どこか我々の感性の深みに持ち続けている心の安らぎとの共鳴である。ラディッチの作品は，今日失われていた良質な建築とは何か，自然と文化の関係性，建築と人間の関係性，その間合いの妙が，本来求められるべき豊かさを慎ましく生みだすことを教えてくれる。

「直角の詩のための家」
この家は，建築家とその家族のための週末住宅として首都サンティアゴから約300キロ南下したビルチェスに建てられている。敷地は近くの国立公園の山々を見渡すことのできる人里離れた広大で豊かな木々に覆われた森の中にある。この住宅とともに建てられた他のスタジオなどのパヴィリオンやプールは，それぞれが点在するように森の中に配置され，独立した場をつくり出し，敷地の自然とともに週末生活を豊かに彩る。

　この家はル・コルビュジエがその晩年，８年の歳月をかけて制作し

The military government following the 1973 *coup d'état* by Pinochet has, until its demise in 1989, caused cultural distortion in Chile, as well as a long period of stagnation in the field of architecture. From the late eighties to the end of his military rule, works of younger-generation architects in their fledgling practice started to gather international attention. Taking the lead was a young Mathias Klotz; then followed architects born around 1965 such as his classmate at the Catholic University in Santiago, capital of Chile, Smiljan Radic, and his junior Alejandro Aravena, who came to achieve global recognition in the 21st century. In the backdrop was a situation where Chile was isolated from the storm of isms, with Postmodernism at the top of the list, that took the international world of architecture of the time, which allowed the proper future of Modernist principles that had been lost in the meantime to slowly mature. As the world was thrown into chaos in its desperate effort to seek a new direction, the body of works by these young Chilean architects has become an international topic that evolved from locality.

Smiljan Radic has worked on numerous residential projects from his earlier career, but his existence came to be rapidly known at home and abroad with his installation at the Venice Biennale 2010, the 2014 Serpentine Gallery Pavilion in London, and his winning proposal for the antenna tower competition in Santiago in 2014. His works have various facets that are sometimes poetic and literary, philosophical and concep-

tual, geometrical, sculpturesque or picturesque; always backed up by the 'skill' of his design full of knowledge and imagination, rich and varied spaces are created through carefully-built relationships with key phenomena that surround the architecture. The rich properties of his spaces are nothing like those that can be acquired through new, special types of experiences; they are resonant with the peace of mind that we always have somewhere deep inside our sensitivity. Radic's works teach us about quality architecture nowadays lost, and show how relationships between nature and culture, relationships between architecture and humans, and the delicacy of these relationships' spacing and timing quietly create the rich properties that ought to be pursued.

House for the Poem of the Right Angle
This is a house built in Vilches, some 300 kilometers south of Santiago, for the architect and his family as a weekend retreat, amid the vast, lush forest in seclusion with a sweeping view over the mountains of the nearby National Park. Elements such as the pavilion housing the studio and the swimming pool that accompany the house are scattered around the forest, each creating a place of its own, showcasing weekend life with the site's natural setting.

The design was inspired by a lithograph from the series *The Poem of the Right Angle* that Le Corbusier has created over the course of eight years in his later life. Taking its cue from

House for the Poem of the Right Angle

たリトグラフのセット，「直角の詩」の1枚の版画にインスパイアされて設計されている。この版画の大胆でおおらかな構図からヒントを得た住宅は，この森の中，無数の石を無造作に散りばめたかのごとくインスタレーションがされた場所に建っている。このストーン・ガーデンのインスタレーションは建築家の夫人であり，協働することの多い彫刻家マルセラ・コレアによる。

施工者はコンクリート造をこの住宅で初めて手がけたのだが，その立体的な外壁は，良い意味で荒々しい仮枠材のパターンを残したものである。その外壁はコンクリートの素材感を消し去るかのように黒く塗られて，ブルータルな表現になりがちな荒々しさと量感を弱め，適度な抽象化がなされている。直線的でエッジの立った面と緩やかにカーブする曲面が組み合わされたヴォリュームは外部に向けてあまり開口部が与えられず，外観の印象は森の中にあって，周囲のストーン・ガーデンに演出された特異な存在であるが，多くを主張せず控えめで静的な存在である。

多くの森に建つ別荘建築が意図するような外部に広がる自然や風景を建物内部に積極的に取り込み一体化させるような仕掛けはここにはなく，むしろ限定された外部の事象を取り込む装置としての開口だけが付けられている。この住宅を立体的に特徴づけているフジツボのよ

うに先細りする造形の三つのスカイライトは様々な方向に向けられて屋根や壁から突き出され，それらだけは外部との交流を積極的に求めているかのようなジェスチュアが与えられている。南北にそれぞれ配置された比較的大きな二つのガラス戸は，建物の外形からはみ出すようなスティールフレームの中をスライドするもので，抽象的な外観において唯一明快な建築的エレメントであり，開閉することで建物の表情を変えることができる。敷地は東から西に向かって緩やかに傾斜しており，その高低差によって一層の建物であるにもかかわらず，この外に向けて開けられた2箇所の開口部は地面に対してのレベルが異なっている。食堂と台所の間のガラス戸は地面レベルにあり，南に広がるストーン・ガーデンの風景を取り込むとともに，第二の玄関／勝手口として機能し，一方，西側寝室にあるガラス戸は空中に浮かび，眼前に広がる木々の風景を内部に取り込んでいる。

内部の空間構成は，中央の中庭とそれを取り囲んだ台所，食堂，居間，寝室を緩やかにつないだ一室空間の居室，玄関背後，寝室の奥に置かれた浴室からなる。建物の南北方向の約半分を占める南側のランプは，壁面同様，黒く塗られている。ランプの終点，西側の二枚の壁と庇に縁取られた玄関に入ると外部の静的な印象から一変した空間が広がる。内部は温かみのある色調の木張りの天井，床，壁と，白壁や

the lithograph's bold and generous composition, the house stands in this forest studded with countless stones; this seemingly random installation is a stone garden created by Marcela Correa, the architect's wife and sculptor who frequently works in cooperation.

While being the first effort in concrete structure on the contractor's part, the house's three-dimensional exterior walls deliberately show falsework patterns that are rugged in a good sense. Painted in black as to erase the concrete texture, the walls' crudeness and sense of volume that tend to be brutal in expression are diminished and abstracted in a moderate manner. A combination of straight-edged surfaces and gentle curves, the volume does not have much openings outward. Its external impression is that of an idiosyncratic presence inside a forest accentuated by the surrounding stone garden, but a succinct and reserved, static one.

Here, unlike many vacation homes built in the woods, gimmicks to bring the surrounding nature and landscape into the building and integrate them are nowhere to be found; instead, the only apertures provided here are devices that introduce exterior events in a very limited manner. Three truncated cone-shaped skylights that characterize this house in a three-dimensional manner jut out from the roof and wall in different directions like barnacles. They are exclusively provided with gestures that look as if seeking interaction with the outdoors. Two comparatively large glazed doors installed on south and

north slide inside steel frames that run over the building's contour as the only clearly architectural element within the abstract appearance that can change the building's expression by opening/closing. With the site gently sloping from east to west, the difference in height causes these two apertures to open outward on different levels with respect to the ground even though the building itself is single-storied. The one between the dining room and the kitchen is on ground level: it introduces the view of the stone garden that stretches southward and functions as a secondary entrance/back door. On the other hand, the one in the bedroom on the west floats in the air, introducing the wide expanse of forest landscape to the inside.

The interior spatial composition involves a courtyard in the center, an open-plan living space surrounding it where the kitchen, dining room, living room and bedroom are loosely connected, and the bathroom placed behind the entrance, at the end of the bedroom. Occupying about half of the building's north-south axis, the ramp on the south side is painted black as with the wall surfaces. Stepping inside the entrance framed by the eave and two walls on the west side at the end of the ramp, one is greeted by an expansive space that dramatically contradicts the static outward impression. Inside is a combination of wood-covered ceiling, floor and wall in warm hues, white wall and concrete wall and floor. In the central courtyard, floor-to-ceiling glass wall partitions the inside from the

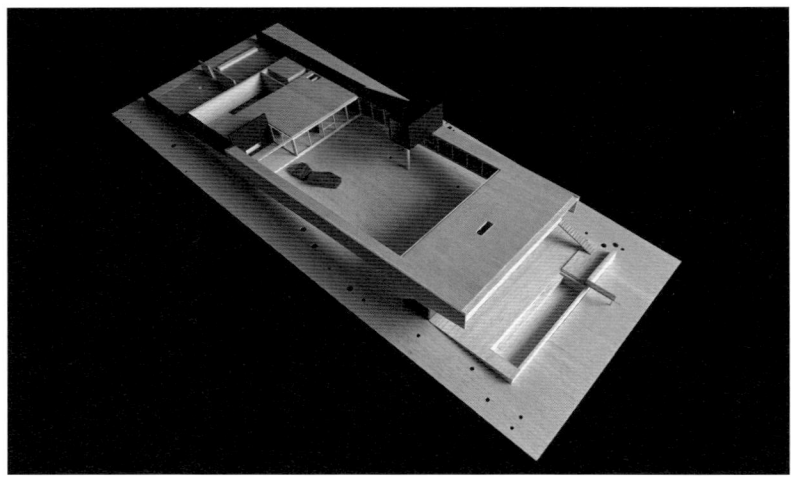
Red Stone House

コンクリートの壁と床の組み合わせで構成される。中央の中庭は天井高いっぱいのガラス壁で内外が仕切られ、4本の既存の木々が生えるこの坪庭のような小さな風景は、その上部に見ることができる外の森に広がる高い木立の緑の遠景とともに内部空間と一体化されている。中庭の出入口となるガラス戸は前述外部の2枚のガラス戸と同様、幾何学的操作によって得られた角度をガラス壁面に対して付けられて、斜めに突き出された方形のスティールフレームの中をスライドする。一室の空間は交互に現れる木とコンクリートの床によってリズムが与えられ、異なる性格の場に切り分けられている。玄関から反時計回りに、シンプルな台所、食堂を進む先に居間がある。傾いた白い丸柱と、壁面と天井からのびる白いスカイライトがつくる壁の表現的なパターン、天井から吊り下げられた木と鉄のコンビネーションの暖炉、そして夫人の二つの彫刻——空中を舞う流体的な木の彫刻と、マッシブであるものの布の柔らかな質感に温かみを感じる彫刻。それらがこの空間に内省的で美しい時間をつくり出し、一対のスカイライトから森の緑が降り注いでいる。

寝室は夫婦と子供たち、計三つのベッドが置かれ、それぞれに白壁に縁取られる外部が当てられている。夫婦のベッドは前述のガラス戸に向けて配置され、木々の風景と向き合い、子供たちの寝床にはスカ

イライトから自然光がもたらされる。

「レッド・ストーン・ハウス」
サンティアゴの高級住宅地の一角に建つ。哲学者の施主は今後30年を家族と暮らすための家を建築家に要望した。この辺りは急速に開発が進んでおり、さほど遠くない近所にも5階建のマンションが建ち、プライバシーの確保が一番の課題であった。

敷地は東側の前面道路に短辺が接した東西に長い長方形であり、西に向かって緩やかに傾斜している。住宅はこの敷地形に相似した長方形の平面を持つことになった。基本構成は短辺に二つの棟——東、道路側の居間／食堂棟と西側の寝室棟——とそれらを結んで長辺を形づくる2本の廊下、そして南側廊下の途中に持ち上げられた書斎からなり、長方形の内側は庭となっている。プライバシー確保のために、住宅は南北、東辺、外部に向けての開口は無く、内部の主要空間は中央に広がる庭に向けられている。緑豊かで外部と遮断された庭は西に向かって下っていき、地面より持ち上げられた寝室棟の下をくぐるように西側のプールまで広がっている。庭には40年前に植えられた30メートルの高さの大木が立ち、加えて植栽された草木に彩られ、言わば大都会のオアシスのような豊かさが獲得されている。この住宅の主空間はこ

outside. The miniature landscape of this spot garden with four existing trees is integrated to the interior space together with the distant view of verdant canopy of trees of the expansive forest that is visible above it. In analogy with the two aforementioned external glazed doors, the one providing access to the inner courtyard is given an angle derived by geometric manipulation with regard to the glass wall, and slides inside the square-shaped steel frame that juts out aslant. Alternate appearance of wooden and concrete floors adds rhythm to the open-plan space, cutting it up into places of different character. Counterclockwise from the entrance, the simple kitchen leads to the dining room that continues into the living room. Expressive pattern on the wall created by the white, leaning round column and the white skylight that stretches from the wall and ceiling; the fireplace, a combination of wood and steel, hanging from the ceiling; and two pieces of sculptures by the wife—a fluid wooden one floating in the air and another massive one with warm texture of soft fabric—all of these contribute to the self-reflective, graceful time that fills this space. The green of the forest pours down from the pair of skylights.

Inside the bedroom are three beds for the couple and their children respectively. The exterior is framed by white walls and allocated to each bed: the couple's bed faces the aforementioned glazed door framing the forest landscape, while the children's bed enjoys some natural light from the skylight.

Red Stone House
The house stands in an upscale residential area of Santiago. The philosopher client asked the architect for a home to live in with his family for three decades to come. The vicinity is undergoing rapid development, and with the recent addition of a five-storied apartment complex built not far away, protection of privacy was on top of the agenda.

A rectangular plot of land stretching along the east-west axis, the site's shorter side touches the front road on the east side, while its ground gently inclines toward west. Eventually the house was given a rectangular floor plan similar to the site's shape. Its basic composition consists of two wings—the living/dining room wing on the east by the road and the bedroom wing on the west—with a pair of corridors connecting the wings that form a rectangle and a study raised over the southern corridor. Inside the rectangle is the garden. For the sake of privacy, the house is devoid of outward openings on its southern, northern and eastern sides. Its main internal spaces face the expansive garden in the center. Rich in green and cut off from the outside, the garden slopes down eastward, passes under the bedroom wing raised above ground, and stretches to the swimming pool on the west side. A 30-meter-tall tree planted 40 years ago hovers over the garden. Supplemented with additional vegetation, the garden achieves the rich quality of an urban oasis. It is the primary space of this house: the living and dining rooms, study and bedrooms are all adjacent to

の庭であり，居間や食堂，書斎や寝室は，庭と常に隣り合い，庭の植物群の演じる美しい風景と，そのたっぷりとした空間の量の恩恵を享受している。

東側道路に沿って前庭とカーポートが配置され，その背後に続くサービス・コートヤードや台所などの使用人ゾーンとともに道路側からの喧騒を防ぐバッファーとなっている。前庭から南辺の廊下の端部にある玄関を入ると，広い庭とそれを囲む諸室，書斎，この住宅の全てが目に飛び込んでくる。玄関の右手の居間と食堂，南辺の廊下はいずれも天井高いっぱいのガラス壁で庭と接している。

居間と食堂はシンプルな方形の一室空間であり，その間は巨大な石のパーティションによって緩やかに分けられている。石のパーティションは垂直軸で回転できるようになっていて，居間と食堂の関係をパフォーマティブに変えることができるものである。食堂の北側のテラスには，チリの住宅に必ず見られるバーベキュー用のグリルが配置される。このテラスから寝室棟に延びる北辺の外部の廊下は南側の廊下と同様，庭の傾斜と反対に緩やかに西に向かって上がっていく。

書斎は庭の中心に配置され，廊下に沿った片持ちの階段を登る2階に配置されている。主人が仕事をするこの空間は日常の暮らしのレベルより持ち上げることで隔離される。円柱で支持されたコンクリート

の方形ヴォリュームの東西壁面は書架で閉じ，南北側をガラス壁とし，机から庭と住宅全体を俯瞰する眺めが与えられている。

寝室棟は中央の廊下に沿って東西側に寝室や家族室，浴室などがシンプルにかつ機能的に並べられる。東西側の壁面は帯状の窓の下には腰壁が与えられ，庭からのプライバシーを確保している。庭は寝室棟下のピロティを潜るように下っていき，プールが配置された西側の庭に至る。西側の庭には芝生が敷き詰められ，子供たちの遊び場となっている。

プログラムや主題も異なるこの二つの住宅に共通することは，実現している様々な空間がもたらす体験が，忘れかけていた感性の深度に響くことである。スタイリッシュに表層的で騒がしく彩度の高い刺激とは全く違う，静かな，半透明で流体的，彷徨う気体のように心に入ってくる感覚。自然の移ろいを受容して，建築と人間の関係性の距離を絶えず変化させ，慎ましく住み手を刺激し続ける家である。

---

the garden and enjoy the benefits of the garden's beautiful scenery full of plants and its ample volume of space.

A front yard and a carport are arranged along the road on the east side to provide a buffer area to block street noise together with the employee zone behind, including the service courtyard and the kitchen. As one enters the front door at the end of the south corridor from the front yard, the vast garden, various rooms surrounding it, the study—the entirety of this residence jump to the eye at once. The living and dining rooms on the right hand side of the entrance as well as the southern corridor are both adjacent to the garden through a floor-to-ceiling glass wall.

The dining and living rooms are accommodated in an open-plan space, loosely separated by a huge stone partition. The latter revolves around the perpendicular axis, for the purpose of transforming the relationship between the living and dining rooms in a performative manner. On the northern side of the dining room is a terrace equipped with a barbecue grill that is essential in Chilean homes. Much like the southern corridor, the external corridor on the north side that stretches from this terrace toward the bedroom wing gently slopes up westward contrary to the garden's inclination.

Placed in the middle of the garden, the study occupies the second level, up the cantilevered stairs installed along the corridor. Isolation is achieved by lifting up this client's work space above the level of everyday living. Supported on a col-

umn, the square-shaped concrete volume is closed on the east and west with bookshelves, whereas its south and north sides are glass walls offering a view of the garden and the entire house from a higher perspective while sitting at the desk.

Inside the bedroom wing are bedrooms, family rooms and bathrooms arranged on the eastern and western sides of a hallway in the middle in a simple yet functional manner. Walls on the east and west feature strip windows above the wainscot that maintains privacy from the garden. The garden passes under the pilotis beneath the bedroom wing and reaches the western garden accommodating the swimming pool. The lawned western garden caters to the children as a playground.

One thing that is common to these two houses that differ both in program and subject theme is that the experience offered by the variety of spaces that are achieved echoes to the forgotten depth of our senses. A far cry from stylish, superficial and clamorously color-intense stimuli, it is a quiet, translucent and fluid feeling that enters our mind like drifting smoke. The house accepts the transitions of nature, constantly changing the distance in the relationship between architecture and humans, and continues to modestly inspire the inhabitants.

English translation by Lisa Tani

*House for
the Poem of the Right Angle*
2010-12

View from south. Entry ramp on right

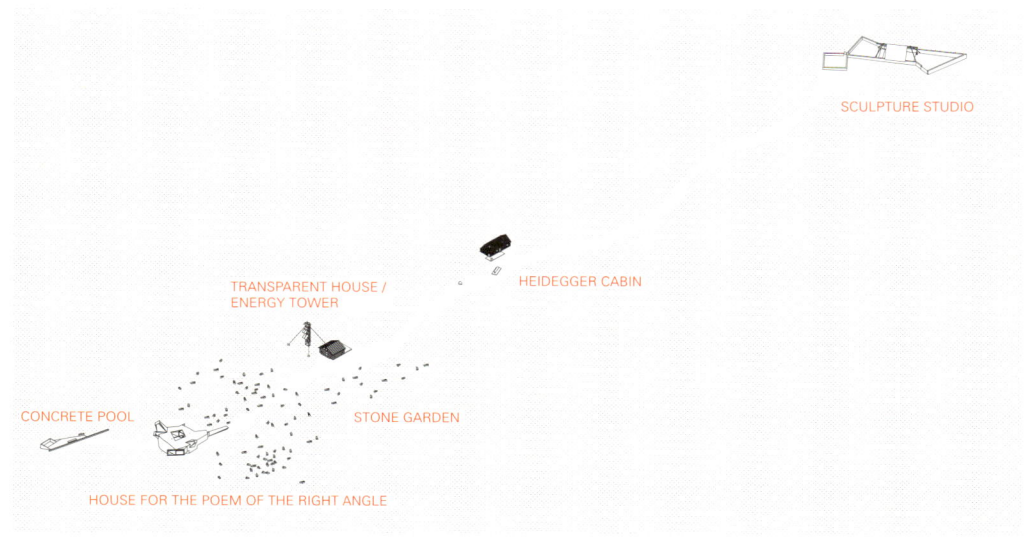

SCULPTURE STUDIO

TRANSPARENT HOUSE /
ENERGY TOWER

HEIDEGGER CABIN

CONCRETE POOL

STONE GARDEN

HOUSE FOR THE POEM OF THE RIGHT ANGLE

Site

1.CONCRETE POOL

2. HOUSE FOR THE POEM OF THE RIGHT ANGLE

3. STONE GARDEN

4. TRANSPARENT HOUSE / ENERGY TOWER

5. STONE SCULPTURE

6. HEIDEGGER CABIN

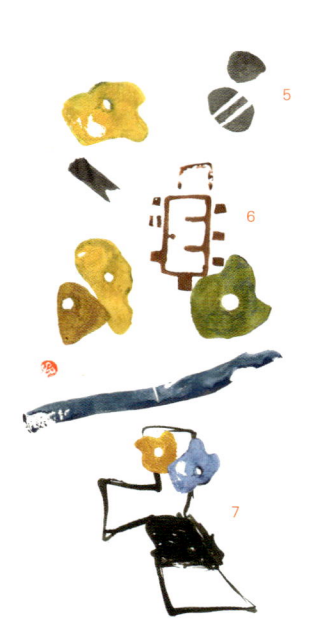

Context

7. SCULPTURE STUDIO

14

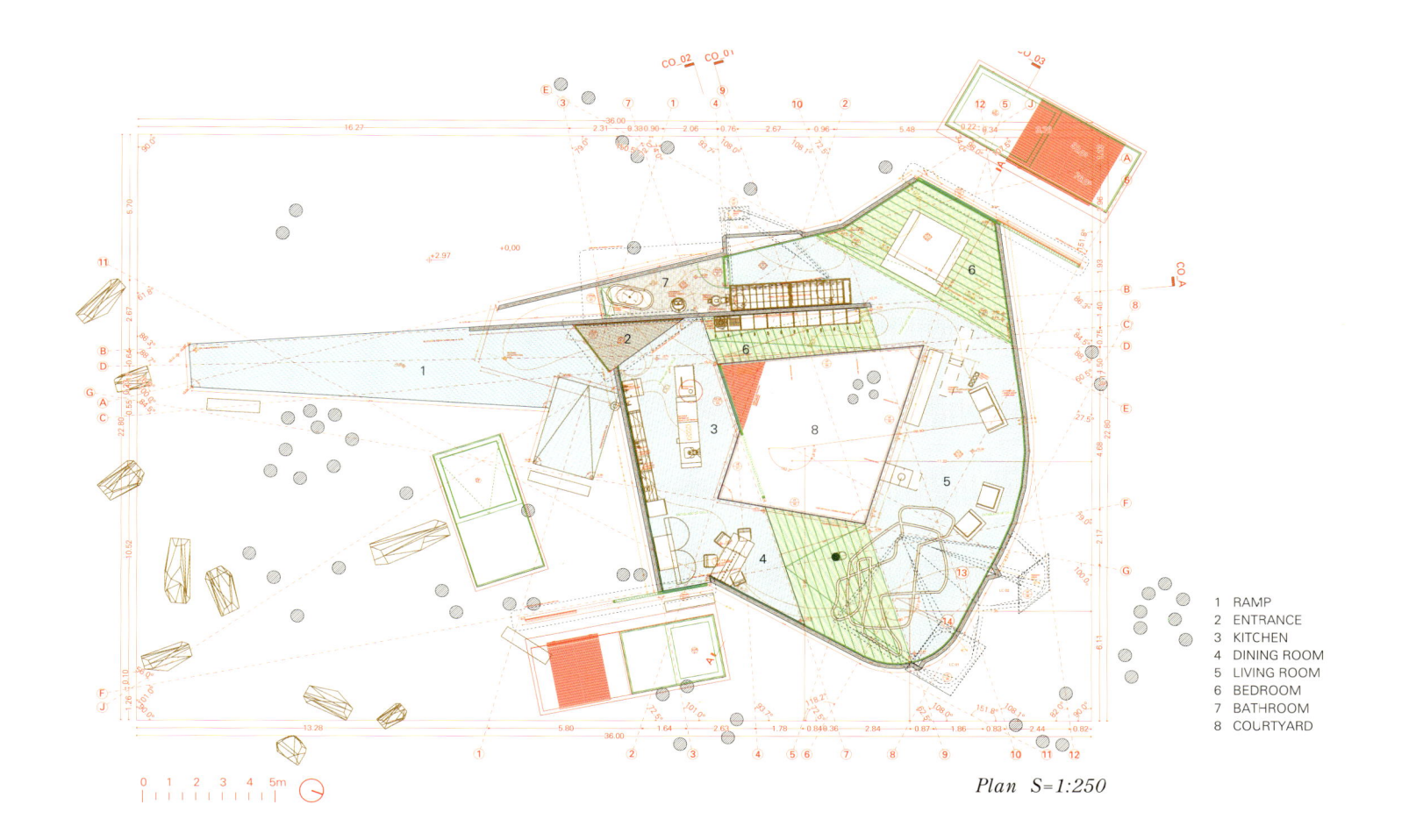

1 RAMP
2 ENTRANCE
3 KITCHEN
4 DINING ROOM
5 LIVING ROOM
6 BEDROOM
7 BATHROOM
8 COURTYARD

Plan S=1:250

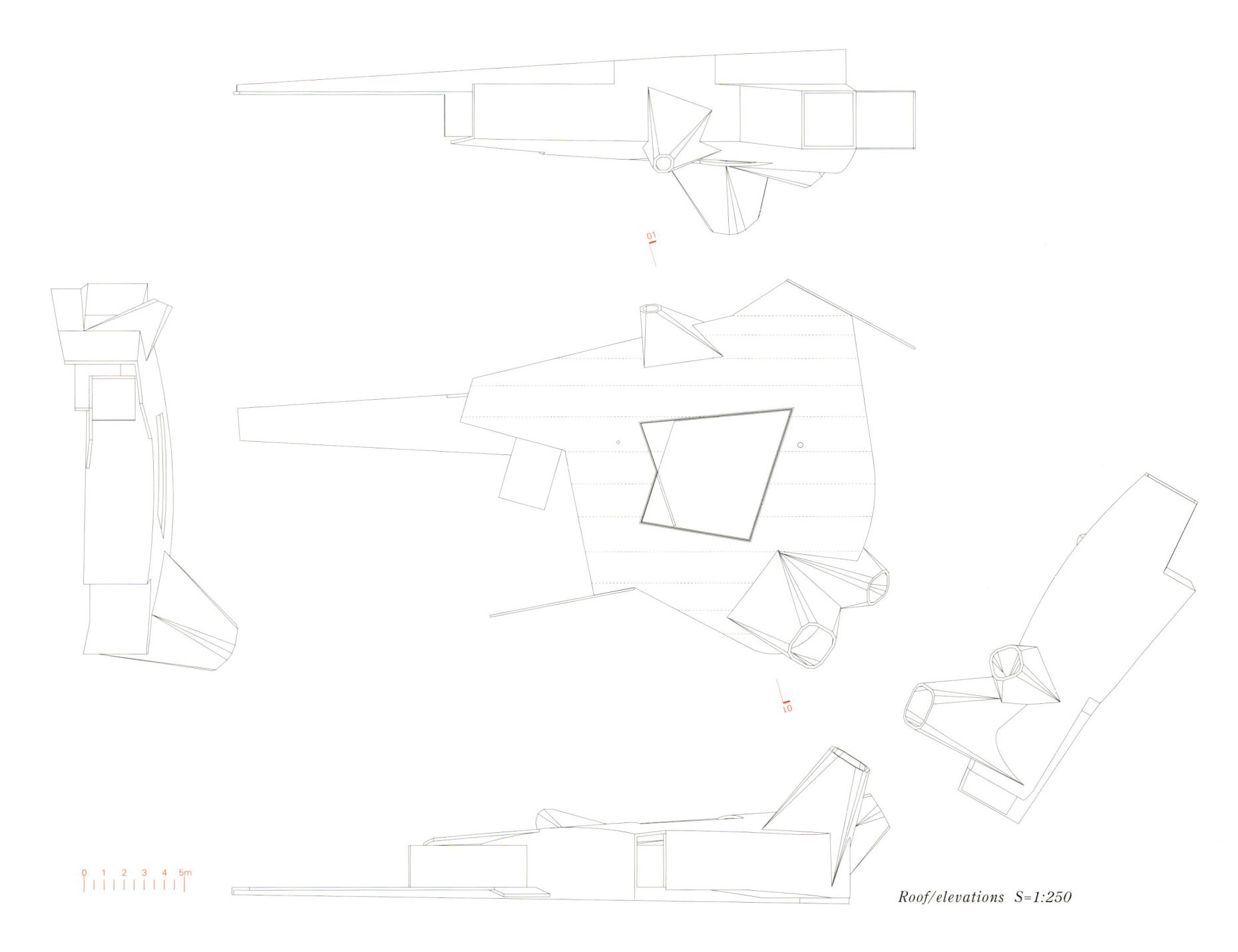

Roof/elevations S=1:250

15

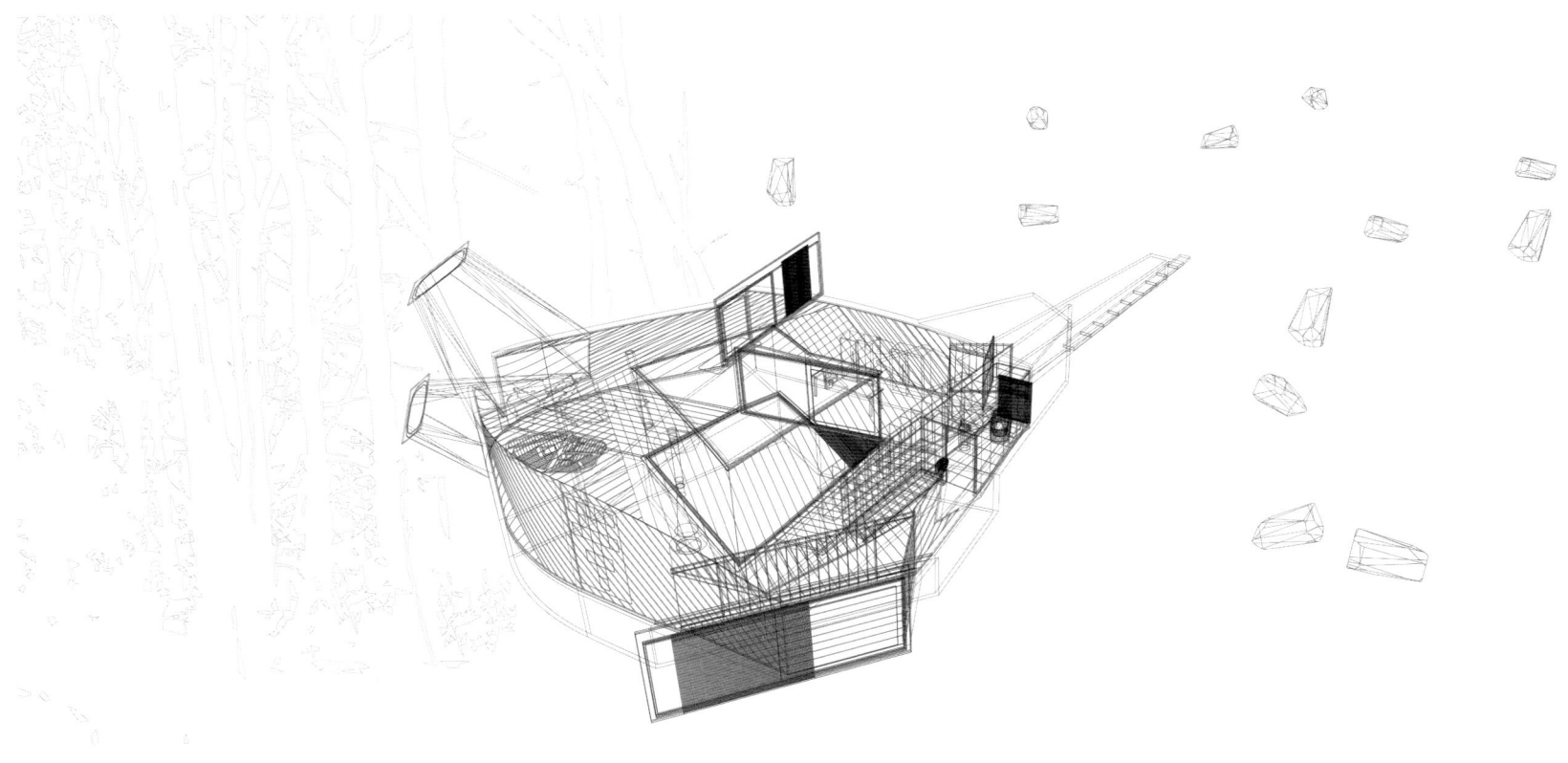

Axonometric

Sketches

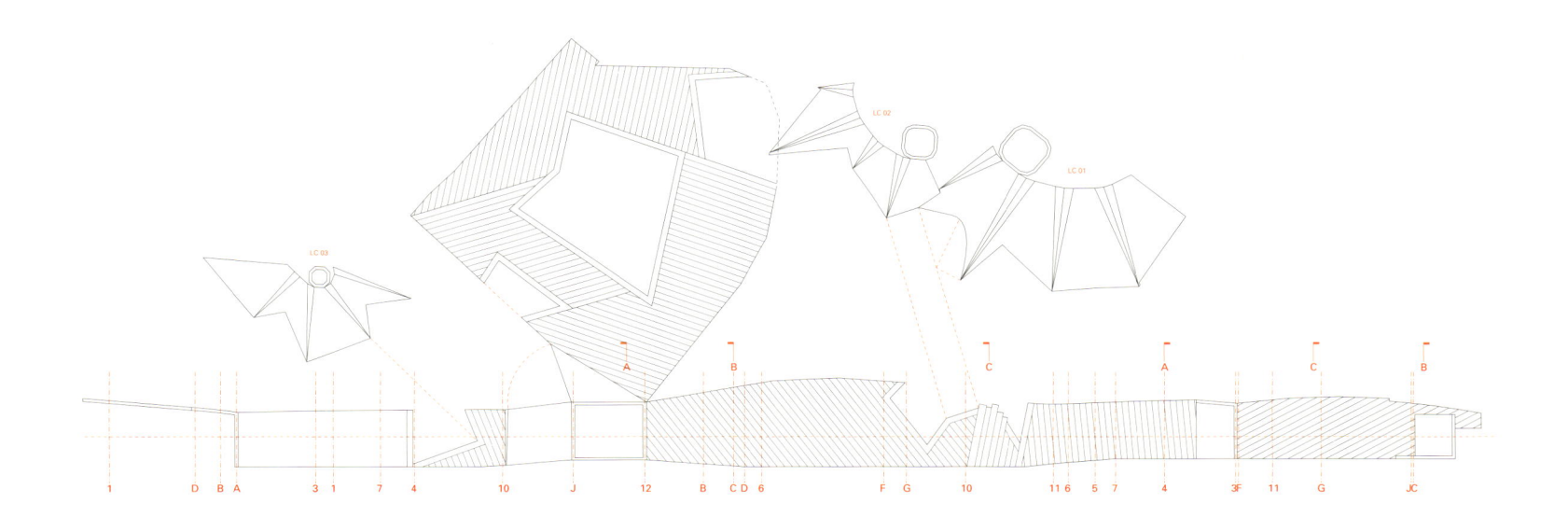

Exploded concrete walls and slab

View from southwest

View from west. Projected skylight for bedroom

View from west. Sliding glass window of bedroom

Terrace of pool and outdoor kitchen/dining

Terrace

Outdoor kitchen

Mountain view from terrace

East elevation. Sliding door of kitchen and skylight for living room

Two skylights for living room

View from southeast

View toward entrance through steel frame of sliding door

31

Ramp: view toward entrance

Ramp: entrance on left

Entrance

Courtyard: kitchen (left) and living room (right)

Courtyard: sliding window setting diagonaly. View from kitchen toward living/dining room

Courtyard: view toward kitchen

Kitchen

Dining room. View toward living room

Living room. Art works by Marcela Correa

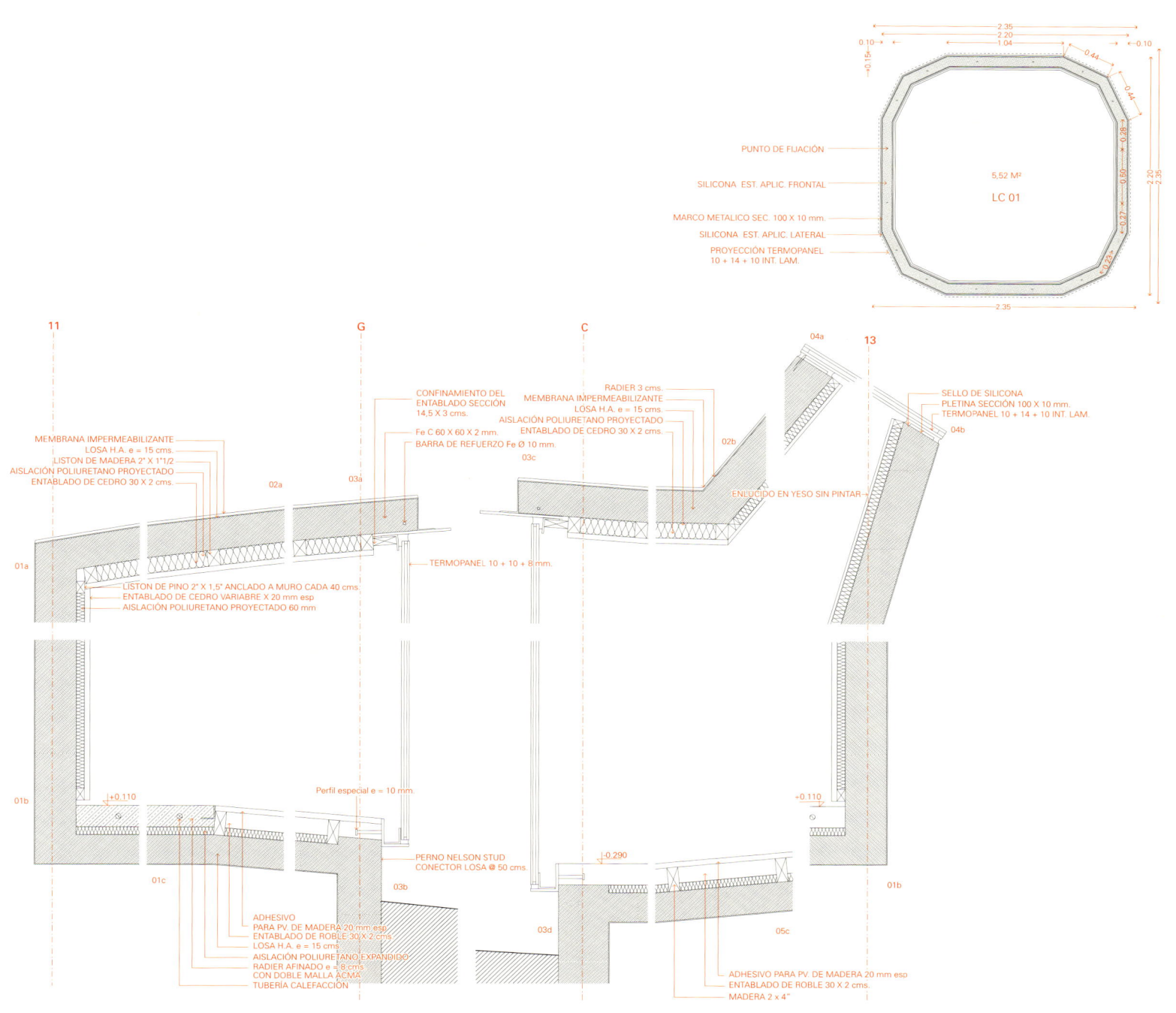

PUNTO DE FIJACIÓN

SILICONA EST. APLIC. FRONTAL

MARCO METALICO SEC. 100 X 10 mm.
SILICONA EST. APLIC. LATERAL
PROYECCIÓN TERMOPANEL
10 + 14 + 10 INT. LAM.

5,52 M²

LC 01

MEMBRANA IMPERMEABILIZANTE
LOSA H.A. e = 15 cms.
LISTON DE MADERA 2" X 1"1/2
AISLACIÓN POLIURETANO PROYECTADO
ENTABLADO DE CEDRO 30 X 2 cms.

CONFINAMIENTO DEL
ENTABLADO SECCIÓN
14,5 X 3 cms.

Fe C 60 X 60 X 2 mm.
BARRA DE REFUERZO Fe Ø 10 mm.

RADIER 3 cms.
MEMBRANA IMPERMEABILIZANTE
LOSA H.A. e = 15 cms.
AISLACIÓN POLIURETANO PROYECTADO
ENTABLADO DE CEDRO 30 X 2 cms.

SELLO DE SILICONA
PLETINA SECCIÓN 100 X 10 mm.
TERMOPANEL 10 + 14 + 10 INT. LAM.

ENLUCIDO EN YESO SIN PINTAR

LISTON DE PINO 2" X 1,5" ANCLADO A MURO CADA 40 cms.
ENTABLADO DE CEDRO VARIABRE X 20 mm esp
AISLACIÓN POLIURETANO PROYECTADO 60 mm

TERMOPANEL 10 + 10 + 8 mm.

Perfil especial e = 10 mm.

PERNO NELSON STUD
CONECTOR LOSA @ 50 cms.

ADHESIVO
PARA PV. DE MADERA 20 mm esp.
ENTABLADO DE ROBLE 30 X 2 cms.
LOSA H.A. e = 15 cms.
AISLACIÓN POLIURETANO EXPANDIDO
RADIER AFINADO e = 8 cms.
CON DOBLE MALLA ACMA
TUBERÍA CALEFACCIÓN

ADHESIVO PARA PV. DE MADERA 20 mm eso
ENTABLADO DE ROBLE 30 X 2 cms.
MADERA 2 x 4"

Sectional detail S=1:25, 1:50

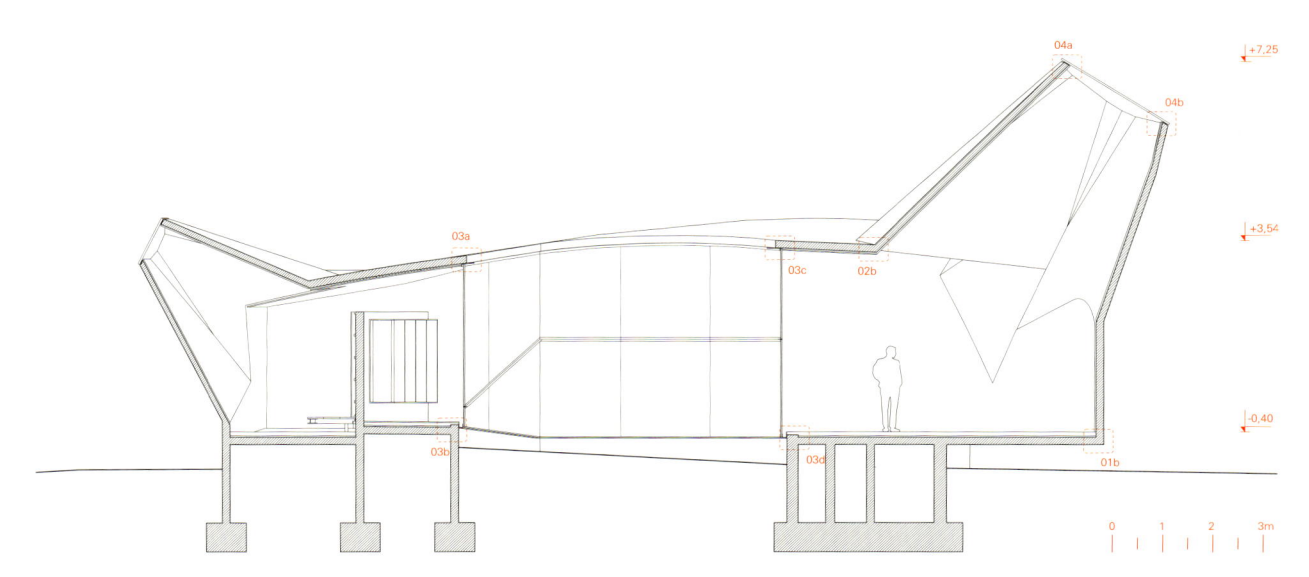

Section S=1:150

Living room

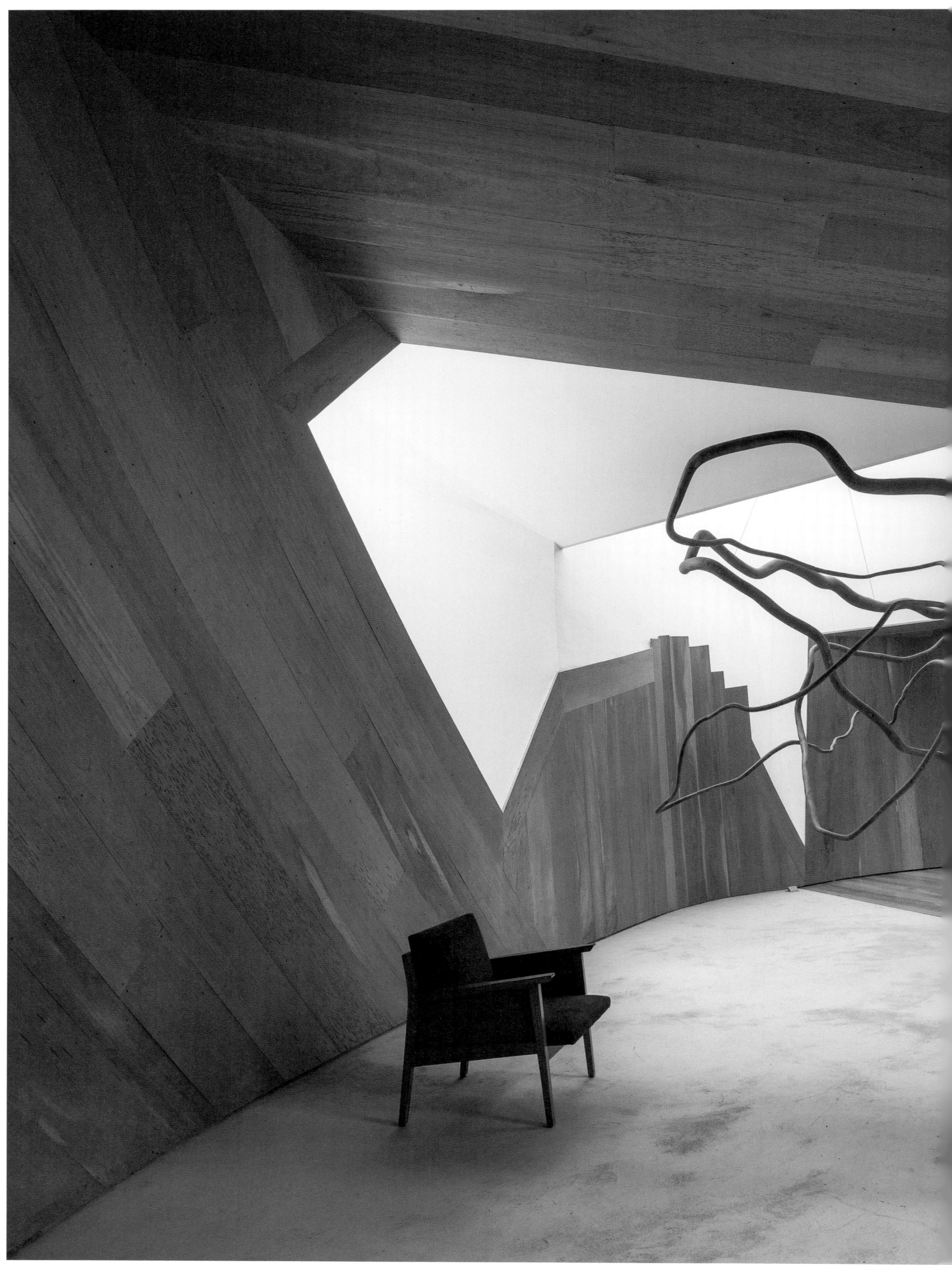

Living room with skylights. Dining room on right

Skylights at living room

Bedroom on west

Bedroom on west

View from bedroom toward living room

Bedroom and children's bedroom

Children's bedroom with skylight. Door of bathroom on center

Skylight at children's bedroom

Bathroom

Skylight at children's bedroom

Energy tower and transparent house (studio)

Transparent house

Transparent house: view of interior

Stone garden and house

Red Stone House 2009-12

Garden: view toward bedroom wing

Garden: view toward dining/living room wing

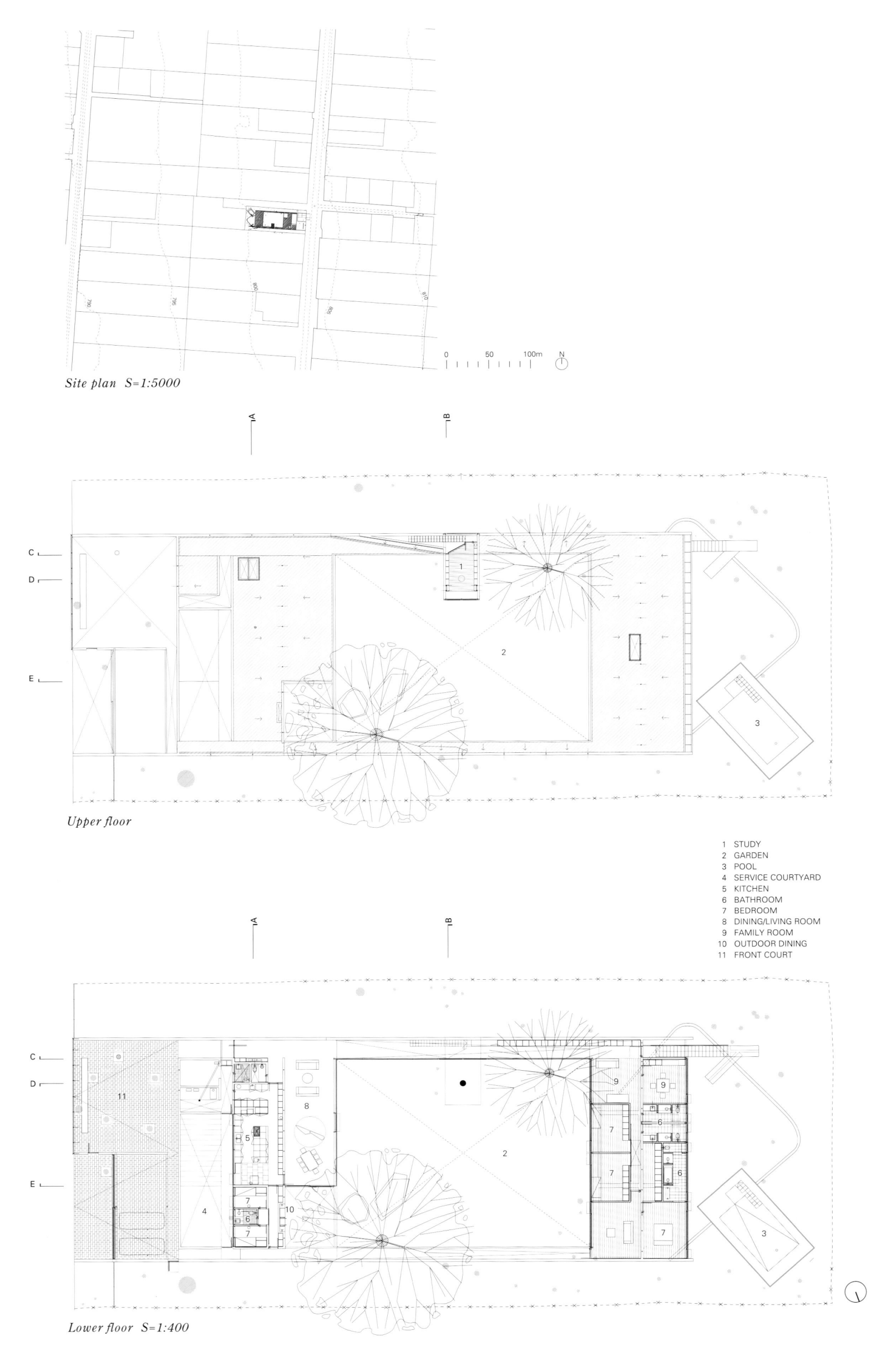

Site plan S=1:5000

Upper floor

1 STUDY
2 GARDEN
3 POOL
4 SERVICE COURTYARD
5 KITCHEN
6 BATHROOM
7 BEDROOM
8 DINING/LIVING ROOM
9 FAMILY ROOM
10 OUTDOOR DINING
11 FRONT COURT

Lower floor S=1:400

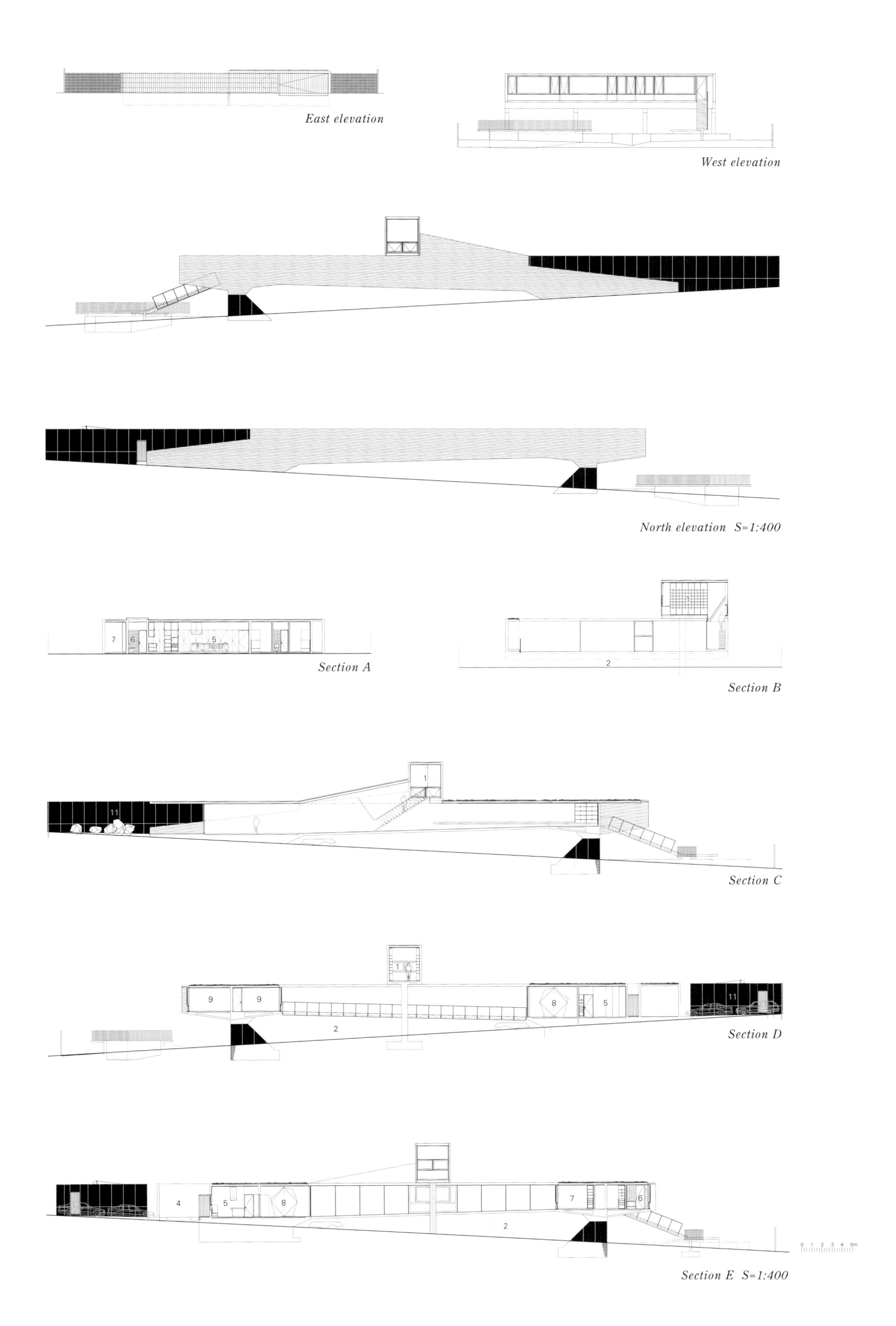

East elevation

West elevation

North elevation S=1:400

Section A

Section B

Section C

Section D

Section E S=1:400

Garden: study on right above

Evening view: outdoor living (left), dining/living room (right)

67

Front court: view toward entrance

Entrance: view toward corridor

View from dining/living room toward garden

Dining/living room. Stone partition on center can be revoluted to change relation of living and dining room

Dining room with stone partition

Stone partition. View toward dining table and outdoor living

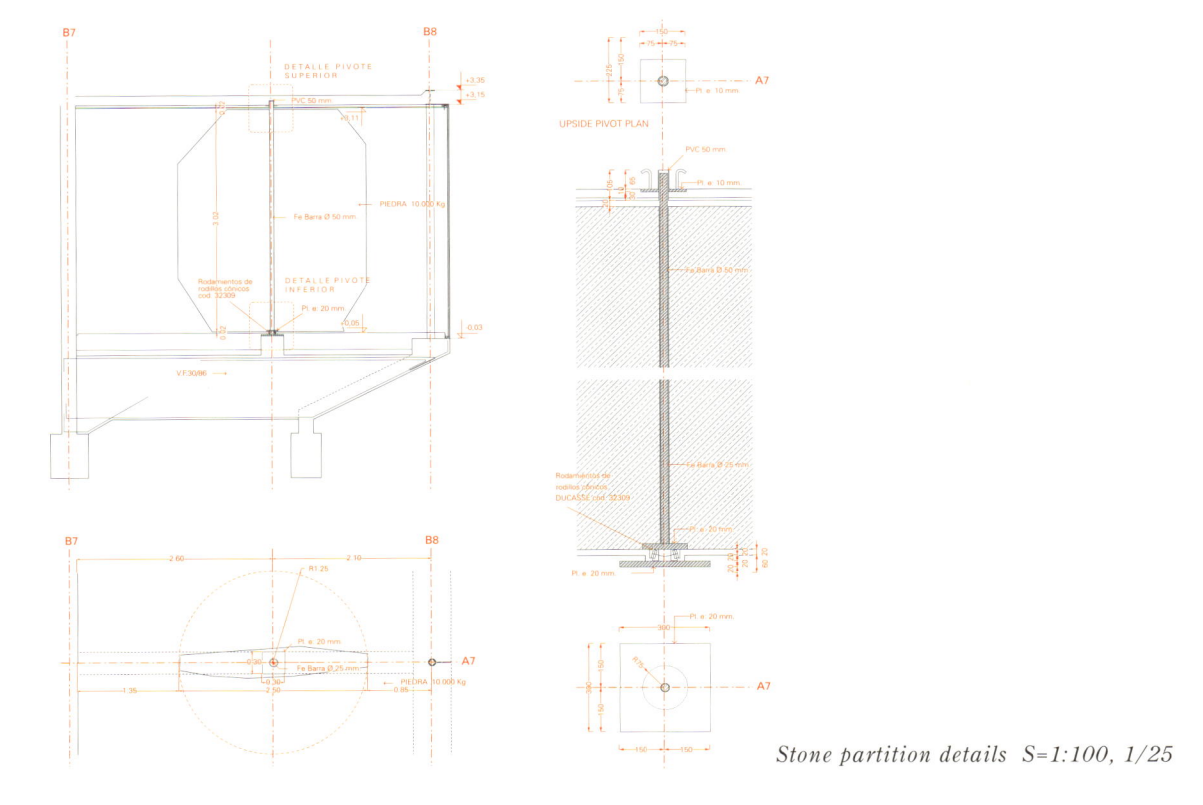

Stone partition details S=1:100, 1/25

Outdoor living, dining room and garden

View toward outdoor living

Ramp connecting bedrooms and dining/living room wing

Corridor: staircase to study

Corridor: staircase to study. View toward entrance

Staircase: view from upper floor

Study

Study: evening view from garden

South elevation

Structural wall supporting bedroom wing

Staircase to bedroom wing from garden

Detail of southwest corner. Staircase to bedroom wing

84

Swimming pool (left) and bedroom wing (right)

MATERIALES

ESTRUCTURA

← 1 HORMIGON A. LISO (MOLDAJE)
← 2 HORMIGON A. LISO PIGMENTADO
← 3 HORMIGON A. BRUTO
← 4 GRANITO
← 5 VOLCOMETAL
← 6 BASE COMPACTADA
← 7 RELLENO
← 8 VIGA H.A.
← 9 ESTRUCTURA MADERA
← 10 ESTRUCTURA METALICA

REVESTIMIENTOS

← 10 REV. ESTUCO
← 11 REV. METALICO
← 12 REV. MADERA
← 13 REV. PIEDRA
← 14 REV. CERAMICO
← 15 REV. VIDRIO MURVI
← 16 REV. M. RECONSTITUIDO (BALDOSA)
← 17 REV. MALLA ELECTROFORJADA
← 18 REV. VOLCANITA
← 19 REV. VOLCAPOL PINTADO

PAVIMENTOS

← 20 PAV. RADIER AFINADO
← 21 PAV. RADIER LAVADO
← 22 PAV. MADERA
← 23 PAV. M. RECONSTITUIDO (BALDOSA)
← 24 PAV. CERAMICO
← 25 PAV. PASTELON H.A. PREFABRICADO
← 26 PAV. MALLA ELECTROFORJADA
← 27 SOBRELOSA HORMIGON LIVIANO
← 28 MORTERO DE PEGA
← 29 HUEVILLO

AISLACION - IMPERMEABILIZACION

← 30 AISLACION ACUSTICA
← 31 POLIESTILENO EXPAND. 100mm.
← 32 POLIESTILENO EXPAND.
← 33 PANEL ISOPOL
← 34 MEMBRANA IMP. S/C
← 35 GEO TEXTIL
← 36 SELLO SILICONA
← 37 CALEFACCION
← 38 POLIETILENO INYECTADO
← 39 LANA MINERAL

CARPINTERIA METALICA

← 40 Fe I IPE 670x150x8x10 m
← 41 Fe I s/calc.
← 42 Pl. e: 5 mm.
← 43 Pl. e: 10 mm.
← 44 Pl. e: 8 mm.
← 45 Fe s/calc.
← 46 Fe 100x100x3 mm.
← 47 Fe 80x40x3 mm.
← 48 Fe 60x40x3 mm.
← 49 Fe Ø s/calc.
← 50 Fe Ø 150x 4 mm.
← 51 Fe Ø 120x4 mm.
← 52 Fe Ø 50x3 mm.
← 53 Fe Ø 75x3 mm.
← 54 Fe C s/calc.
← 55 Fe C 200x50x3 mm.
← 56 Fe C 150x50x4 mm.
← 57 Fe C 100x50x3 mm.
← 58 Fe C 80x40x3 mm.
← 59 Fe L 100x100x4 mm.
← 60 Fe L 65x65x4 mm.
← 61 Fe L 50x50x3 mm.
← 62 Fe L 40x40x3 mm.
← 63 Fe L 30x30x3 mm.
← 64 Fe 20x20x2 mm.
← 65 Grate acero inoxidable
← 66 Fe L 100x100x8 mm.
← 67 Fe 50x20x3 mm.
← 68 Fe C 120x50x4 mm.
← 69 Fe 20x20x2 mm.

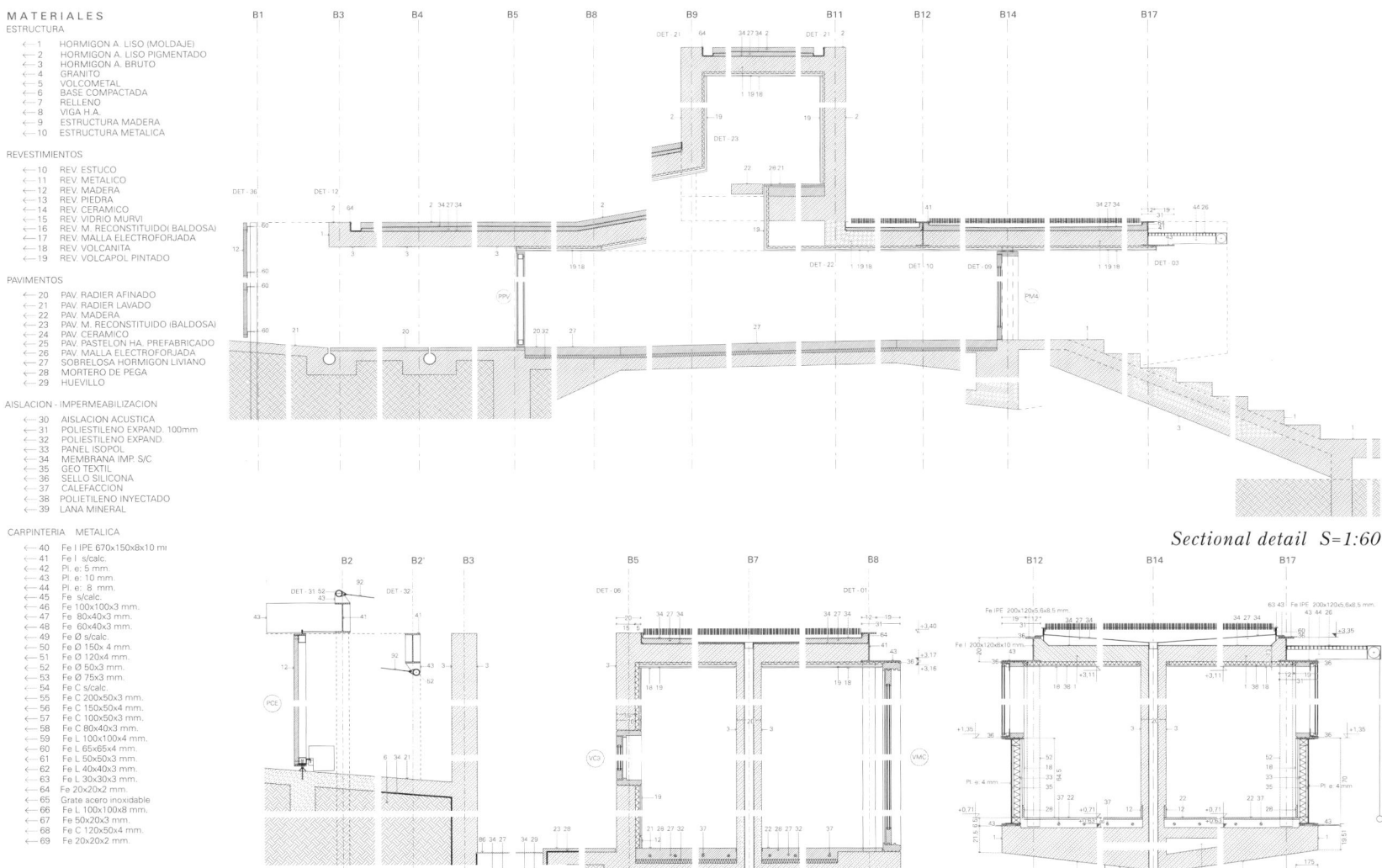

Sectional detail   S=1:60

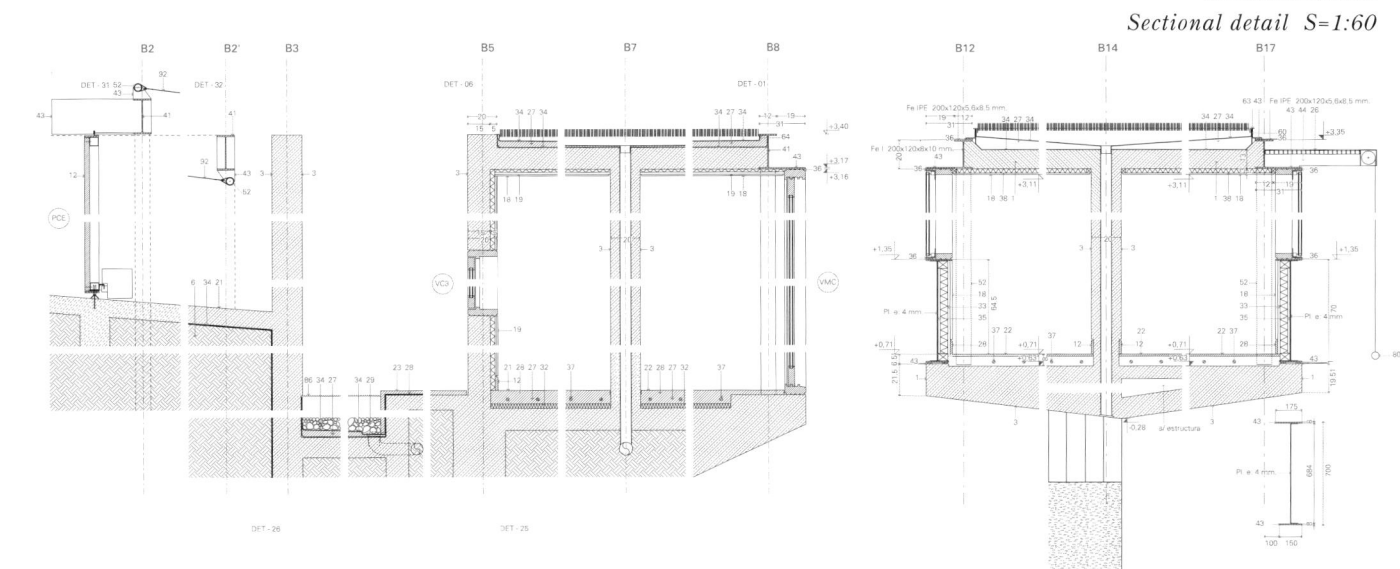

Sectional detail   S=1:50

Garden: view toward dining/living room wing

Photographs are taken by Yoshio Futagawa except as noted below
p.7: © Gonzalo Puga
p.8: courtesy of Smiljan Radic

世界現代住宅全集21
スミリャン・ラディッチ
「直角の詩」のための住宅
レッド・ストーン・ハウス

2016年1月25日発行
撮影・文・編集：二川由夫
アート・ディレクション：細谷巖

印刷・製本：大日本印刷株式会社
制作・発行：エーディーエー・エディタ・トーキョー
151-0051　東京都渋谷区千駄ヶ谷3-12-14
TEL.(03)3403-1581(代)

ISBN 978-4-87140-646-8 C1352